THE MINISTER'S
FILING SYSTEM

by

Paul Gericke

"Let all things be done decently and in order."
I Corinthians 14:40

BAKER BOOK HOUSE
Grand Rapids, Michigan

In Memory of
My Parents
Orville and Irma Gericke

Copyright 1971 by
Paul Gericke
Reprinted 1978 by
Baker Book House

ISBN: 0-8010-3721-2

Library of Congress
Catalog Card Number:
71-181033

First printing, March 1979
Second printing, November 1979

PHOTOLITHOPRINTED BY CUSHING - MALLOY, INC.
ANN ARBOR, MICHIGAN, UNITED STATES OF AMERICA
1979

PREFACE

The Ministers Filing System is based on the Eureka Filing System, which in turn is an adaptation of an old scheme called the Wilson Filing System. The Eureka System has been taught at several large seminaries for many years and used widely by preachers and pastors with effectiveness. The system has been taught by such men as Dr. V. L. Stanfield, Professor of Preaching at the New Orleans Baptist Theological Seminary, and Dr. Hugh R. Peterson, formerly Administrative Dean of the Southern Baptist Theological Seminary. The writer is indebted to these men for instruction in the use of the system.

The writer is especially grateful to Dr. Stanfield for his counsel and suggestions in the writing of the manuscript. He has adapted the Eureka Filing System in his own way and developed it for the use of preachers. He designed the printed sermon folders for storing sermon manuscripts and materials.

The Eureka System has been revised and enlarged by the writer to include files for the use of ministers of education, ministers of music, and other Christian workers; a variation in the use of materials in setting up the system; and a suggested list of subject headings for the index. In addition, a scheme for using the Dewey Decimal Classification for indexing and shelving bound volumes has been provided. Grateful acknowledgment is given to the Forest Press, Inc., for permission to use the Second Summary and the Third Summary of Religion of the Dewey system.

Dr. Harry Eskew, Associate Professor of Music History at the New Orleans Baptist Seminary, has read the manuscript and offered helpful suggestions that have made the Ministers Filing System more useful to ministers of music.

The printed forms and sermon folders may be obtained through the Student Store of the New Orleans Baptist Seminary, 3939 Gentilly Boulevard, New Orleans, Louisiana.

The Ministers Filing System has been designed and published in hope that it will be of help to the many faithful ministers of God in their manifold duties in the world.

CONTENTS

INTRODUCTION

The modern minister is in constant need of materials for his speaking and writing responsibilities. In collecting these materials he needs a simple filing system to store information as it becomes available and to make it easily accessible later. The Ministers Filing System is so designed to fill this need for ministers and other Christian workers.

The ministry today is many-sided, including not only the preacher, the pastor, the evangelist, the professor, the missionary, the denominational leader, and the chaplain, but also the minister of education, the minister of youth, the minister of music, and other Christian workers. These many servants of God need a filing system that is distinctively their own, one that is specifically adapted to their needs. They need a system whereby they can file and index materials on a variety of subjects which they have found through study and observation and at a later date have ready access to these materials in preparation of sermons, speeches, and publications.

A number of filing systems are available to the minister today. Several factors should be considered in the selection of a system most suitable to the minister. First of all, the filing procedure and the system of indexing material should be basically simple, providing the shortest possible way to materials that have been preserved through the years. The system should be essentially mechanical so that anyone can be taught to maintain and operate it for the minister. In addition, the scheme of arrangement should be all-inclusive, having one central index to a variety of files and sources of materials. The system should also be adaptable, for the minister may choose to modify or add on to his system of files in his later ministry with new opportunities of service. Furthermore, it should save him time in locating materials and at the same time require a minimum of time to set up and to maintain in operation. The filing system should also be inexpensive and should make use of standard size materials readily available at book stores and places that handle office supplies.

Most filing systems available today and the many self-made systems are arranged basically on the principle of filing materials according to subject. Articles, clippings, manuscripts, etc. are placed, sometimes stuffed, in manila folders, which often become large and bulky. The number of general subject categories are limited, and no system of cross-reference is used. Many pieces of material can be classified under two or more subjects and are lost to research in certain areas unless some arrangement is made to index the material on all the subjects that they cover at some length. The expense of some systems is prohibitive especially in the minister's early years when the filing system should be set up.

The Ministers Filing System has all the features of an efficient arrangement of files and of indexing materials and sources, and it is most suitable for the Christian worker in a variety of fields of service. Furthermore, it does not have the limitations of other systems, nor does it lack any important features that others may claim.

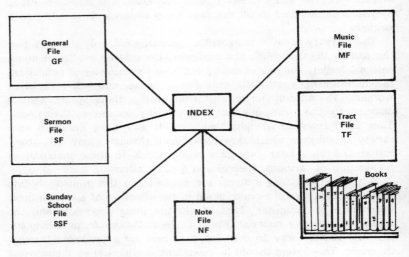

Figure 1

I. THE GENERAL PLAN

The Ministers Filing System is designed to provide a depository and a reference scheme for all of the minister's materials with an index to guide him to these materials at a later date. His materials fall into several categories: (1) articles that can be clipped from newspapers, magazines, and journals; (2) materials from books and bound volumes that cannot be removed and are too long to be copied; (3) notes, quotations, and outlines recorded in the course of reading, meditation, or conversation or in the process of listening to sermons and speeches; and (4) pamphlets, tracts, manuscripts, and mimeographed material gathered from time to time.

The system is composed of several files designed to collect material of a similar nature in a neat and orderly manner with a subject index to direct the minister to these materials as he has need of them. Provision is also made to guide him to references in books and bound volumes. He may have as many files as he feels is necessary, but all the materials are recorded in one central index. He may have files for general materials, notes, sermons, poems, materials of special interest, and periodicals that he choses to keep. His index directs him to any one or several of these files according to the subject of concern at any time (see Figure 1).

Of course the minister should not set up more files than is necessary. He should have at least a General File and a Note File, for these would handle most of his materials. In addition, he should have a scheme for locating references in bound volumes. He should use standard size folders that would handle 8½ by 11 inch materials for all his files except the Note File and the Poem File. He should use 4 by 6 inch cards for the latter two. These may be stored behind the index cards in one file box at first and placed on top of the file cabinet where all the other files are stored, beginning with the General File.

II. THE INDEX

The key to the Ministers Filing System is the Index, which is composed of two parts. The first part is a series of subject cards, alphabetically arranged. These are 4 by 6 inch index cards, readily obtained from stores that handle office supplies. One method of indexing is to obtain ruled index cards and divide them in half with a vertical line with the subject indicated in the upper left hand corner (see Figure 2). Each entry is typed or printed on a half line, beginning with the upper left line and continuing down the left column until filled. The right column is then used in a similar manner. When the front side is filled, the back of the card may be used, if ruled, or a second card used with the notation "continued" typed in at the top behind the subject notation. Another method is to mimeograph, or have printed, a four column arrangement. Each entry is typed or printed on two quarter lines. Both sides of the card may be used (see Figure 3).

BIBLE – MIRACLES	

Figure 2

ORU LIBRARY

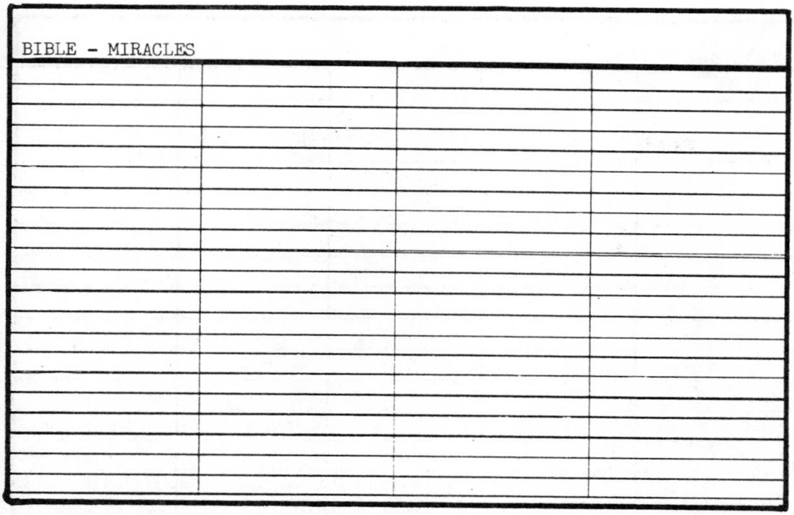

BIBLE - MIRACLES

Figure 3

The first time material is acquired on a particular topic, the subject is typed in capital letters in the upper left hand corner of an index card. For example, in his reading the minister finds an article entitled "The Miracles of the Bible" which he feels he can use at a later time. He needs then to type the subject BIBLE - MIRACLES on an index card. This card will serve as an index to all his materials in his files and in his bound volumes on this particular subject. As materials on other subjects are acquired, index cards are made in a similar way. In the last section of this book, a suggested list of subject headings is provided as a guide to the minister so that he can have uniformity in his index listings.

The second part of the Index is a set of scripture reference cards, which is needful for the preacher of the gospel in sermon preparation but optional for other ministers depending on their need and interest. Index cards are prepared for each of the sixty-six books of the Bible. If ruled index cards are used, five columns are needed on each side or on two cards. These are provided by four equally spaced vertical lines (see Figure 4). Cards may also be mimeographed or printed (see Figure 5). The name of the book of the Bible is typed in the upper left hand corner. Each column provides spaces for various chapters of the book to be indexed. The first column is for chapters ending in 1, that is, chapters 1, 21, 31, etc., the second for chapters ending in 2, that is, 2, 22, 32, etc., and so on until the tenth column for chapters ending in 0. Each line in the column provides space for the specific chapter and verse numbers and the specific file numbers. This set of index cards should be placed directly behind the subject index cards in the file box.

GENESIS				

Figure 4

GENESIS														
Ch.	V.	Ref.	Ch.	V.	Ref.	Ch.	V.	Ref.	Ch.	V.	Ref.	Ch.	V.	Ref.

Figure 5

III. THE GENERAL FILE

The Index of the Ministers Filing System directs the minister to a set of files. The General File is used as a depository for materials of a general nature, except for very small clippings. This includes articles and editorials taken from newspapers, magazines, and journals that the minister does not intend to keep and also manuscripts, typescripts, mimeographed materials, brochures, bulletins, and pamphlets. If the articles are small or odd shaped, they should be pasted on 8½ by 11 inch sheets of white paper for uniformity.

The file itself is a set of manila file folders measuring 9 by 12 inches with either a three-cut or five-cut index tab. Each folder can handle twenty-five pieces of material with ease. Thus, the first folder receives the first twenty-five clippings or other materials and is labeled GF 1-25 either by printing on the index tab or by typing a label and gluing it on the tab (see Figure 6). The next folder is labeled GF 26-50, and each successive folder includes the next twenty-five numbers.

The first piece of material to be filed is marked with the notation GF1 in the upper right hand corner of the long side of the paper, i.e., the 11 inch side of an 8½ by 11 inch sheet. The subject heading or headings are printed in the upper left hand corner. Each piece of material can usually be classified under at least two headings, sometimes more. For example, an editorial from *The Watchman-Examiner*, Feb. 25, 1965, entitled "Unless You Repent," is to be filed in the General File. The page on which the article is printed is torn out of the periodical carefully. Since the page is about 8½ by 11 inches, it fits nicely in the folder. The page is turned with the right side up and the top of the page to the left, and the file number GF1 is printed in the upper right hand corner and the subjects REPENTANCE and EVANGELISM in the upper left hand corner, one under the other. The margins usually provide enough room for these markings. The page is then ready to be indexed and placed in the front of the file. The next clipping is labeled in a similar fashion with file number GF2 and the proper subject headings and then indexed and placed behind the first article (see Figure 6). This process is continued until twenty-five pieces of material are filed, and then another file folder is used with the first clipping marked GF26 and so on.

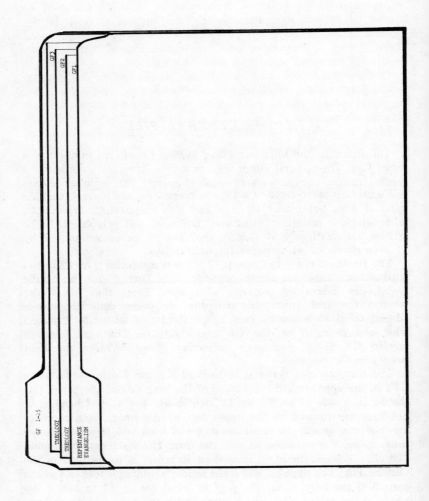

Figure 6

OSU LIBRARY

As materials are collected from time to time, they should be labeled by subject immediately while the content is fresh in the minister's mind. They should be set aside in a folder marked "To Be Filed." Every two weeks or more when a number of materials have been collected, they should be given file numbers, then recorded in the Index, and finally filed away in the proper folder. The minister should guard against over-filing. When he is ready to index his material, he should reflect again over the articles collected and possibly eliminate unnecessary material.

After a number of materials have been collected and classified according to subject and then given a file number, they are ready to be entered into the Index. The notation should have enough information to identify the material but brief enough to be entered in the space provided on the index card. Therefore, the minister should use abbreviations and symbols whenever possible. For example, the index notation for the editorial "Unless You Repent" from *The Watchman-Examiner* is recorded as follows:

REPENTANCE	
GF1 W-E ed. Unless You Repent	

Figure 7

GF1 is the file number, W-E is the symbol for *The Watchman-Examiner,* "ed." is abbreviation for editorial, and of course the title was short enough to enter in full. The same entry should be recorded on an index card labeled EVANGELISM. The author is often important in identifying the material and may be included by abbreviating the last name. For example, the next piece of material to be filed and indexed is a mimeographed copy of a paper entitled "The Layman and Theology" delivered by Dr. Samuel J. Mikolaski to the Layman's Conference at the New Orleans Baptist Theological Seminary in March, 1967. The content is classified under the subjects THEOLOGY and LAYMEN and given the file number GF2, since it is the second piece of material to be filed. The notation on the index card labeled THEOLOGY is as follows:

GF2 mim. Mikol. Layman & Theology

The date may also be important and may be included after the identification for the type of material, as "mim." for mimeographed material, with this notation:

GF2 es.mim. 3/67 Mikol. Lay. & Theo.

The abbreviation "es." stands for essay or paper. Only include such information that will identify the material enough at a later date and indicate whether the material can be used for a particular need. The same notation in the above example should be entered on the index card labeled LAYMEN.

The next entry is classified according to subject and given the file number GF3. For example, an article entitled "Fact and Faith in Modern Theology" by Stephen Board in *Christianity Today,* May 26, 1967, is indexed on the card labeled THEOLOGY after the first entry as follows:

THEOLOGY	
GF2 es.mim. 3/67 Mikol. Lay.&Theo.	
GF3 CT art.Board,Fact&Faith-Mod.Th.	

Figure 8

The symbol CT stands for *Christianity Today* and "art." for article. The same notation should be entered on an index card labeled FAITH. Other entries from the various files are recorded in succession on the index cards as the materials are collected and classified, regardless of their particular file numbers.

IV. THE NOTE FILE

The Note File is another basic necessity of the Ministers Filing System along with the General File. This file is designed to preserve materials that can be entered on a 4 by 6 inch ruled card. This includes small clippings, brief notes and quotations, and short poems. For example, the following notes and quotations were jotted down in the process of reading and later typed on the first card to be collected in the Note File:

```
PRAYER                                                          NF1
                      Prayer Changes Things
        Prayer changes things at the other end and at the praying
   end.
        "When prayer can make any change it likes at the starting
   end, it will make any change you like at the other end." (p.16).
        "When God can reach in His hand and do as He likes with us,
   we can reach out our hands and do as we like with - God" (p.14).




                Five Laws That Govern Prayer by S. D. Gordon
```

Figure 9

The material was classified under the subject PRAYER and given the first number of the Note File NF1. Any pertinent information, especially the specific source reference, should be recorded on the last line.

The subject matter on the note card is then indexed on the card in the Index labeled PRAYER in the following way:

NF1 qu. S.D.Gordon,Pr.ChangesThings

The abbreviation "qu." stands for quotation. The initials are needed with the author's last name because several well known men with this name are associated with Christianity.

The next note card is given the file number NF2. To illustrate, the minister heard some striking statements on repentance by Billy Graham on his "Hour of Decision" broadcast on August 30, 1964. He jotted down a paraphrase of these statements on a piece of scratch paper and later typed these on a note card which he classified under the subject of REPENTANCE, and he gave the card the file number NF2. He took the index card labeled REPENTANCE and made this entry:

REPENTANCE	
GF1 W-E ed. Unless You Repent	
NF2 ser.Graham, Rep.is not..,is...	

Figure 10

The abbreviation "ser." is for sermon, and the notation for the statements indicates that Graham described what repentance is not, and what repentance is. The minister has to decide for himself what notation he gives material that has no title so that at a later date he can recognize its content. These note cards may be taken to the pulpit, and the statements may be read for emphasis or for effect. Then later they should be returned to the file box.

V. THE SERMON FILE

Sermons may be filed and indexed in several ways. If the minister prepares his sermons using notes, he may type or print them on loose leaf note paper and file them in loose leaf binders according to texts in the order that they appear in the Bible. Only the subjects need to be cross-referenced in the subject part of the Index since the sermons are already in Biblical order. The reference to be entered in the Index should include the Sermon File symbol SF, the text of the Bible, and the sermon subject. For example, a sermon on the subject "The Creation of Man", based on Genesis 2:7, is entered on the subject index cards CREATION and MAN as follows:

SF Ge. 2:7 Creation of Man

Only the symbol SF following the chapter and verse numbers are needed on the scripture reference cards of the Index. In the above example the sermon is indexed by the text Gen. 2:7 (See Indexing by Scripture, p. 21). If more than one passage is used as a text, the sermon is filed in the binder according to the first passage, and the others are indexed on the scripture reference cards.

If the minister primarily preaches topical sermons, he would benefit by keeping his notes in file folders similar to the General File. Standard 8½ x 11 inch notebook paper or typing paper should be used. From ten (SF 1-10) to twenty-five (SF 1-25) sermons may be filed in one folder, depending on the average length of the preacher's sermon notes. Sermons receive successive numbers as they are entered in the file folders. If the above sermon is the first to be filed, it receives the notation SF1 and is entered on the index cards MAN and CREATION as follows:

SF1 Creation of Man

The same sermon is also indexed on the scripture reference cards according to the text Gen. 2:7.

If full notes or a full manuscript is utilized by the minister, the best method is to use one folder for each sermon. Materials used in preparation, such as clippings, notes, poems, etc., may also be kept in the file folder. The notation and indexing of the sermon are the same as the above method, the first file folder receiving the symbol SF1, the second file folder SF2, and so forth. The subject and text may be printed on the front of the folder or typed on a label and glued on the front.

Special folders may be prepared by a printer or may be mimeographed with notations and lines on the front of the folder for pertinent information about the sermon. This should include the following information: the subject of the sermon, the title, the text, the scripture reading, the type of sermon according to subject matter and method, the objective of the message, and the source of materials used in preparation. Columns should also be used for indicating the place where the sermon was preached, the date, and the response during the invitation or other effects observed by the preacher. (See Figure 11).

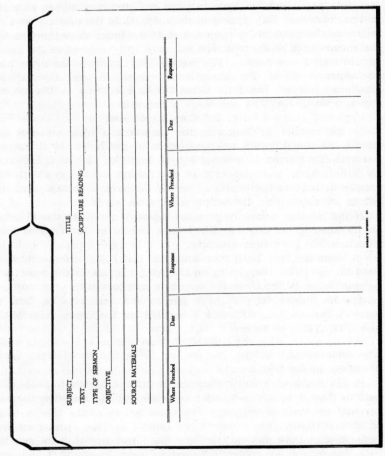

Figure 11

VI. OTHER FILES

Many ministers have specialized fields of service. Some ministers may have a special interest in Sunday school work and desire to keep these materials separate. One method is to set aside a certain group of numbers in the General File for Sunday school materials, such as GF1001 to GF2000. Other groups of numbers may be set aside for special materials. But these groupings should be kept to a minimum, since all the materials are indexed and thus grouped together on the index cards for ready reference.

However, a separate file may be set up for Sunday school materials. A set of file folders similar to the General File may be used and marked SSF for Sunday School File. Thus the folders are marked SSF 1-25, SSF 26-50, etc. The materials are placed in the folders and recorded in the Index as in the system of the General File.

In like manner a Music File may be set up using the symbol MF. Sheet music and scores may be filed with other materials pertaining to music and given a special group of numbers, such as MF1001 to MF2000. These may be kept in file folders or in special folders designed to protect them. Or, a special file may be designed just for them. Whatever the number of files used, all materials should be recorded in the Index. The symbols identify the particular file, and the number identifying the piece of material directs the minister from the Index to the material sought.

A minister may prefer to keep his tracts and pamphlets in a separate file. This may be called the Tract File, identified as TF, and set up similar to the General File. Or, he may prefer to keep tracts on the same subject together. The file folders may be identified by subject, such as TF Sal. for the folder holding the tracts on salvation. The first tract entered is TF Sal.1, the second TF Sal.2, and so forth. These notations with the title of the tract appear in the Index under the subject SALVATION.

Some ministers may prefer to keep a particular journal or magazine, such as *Christianity Today, Christian Century, Church Administration,* or *The Church Musician.* These may be kept in file folders by the year or half year and identified by the first letters of the title, such as CTF for Christianity Today File. Articles in these periodicals are identified in the Index by the file symbol, the date of the issue, the page number, and the title of the article. For example, if the minister chooses to keep his copies of *Christianity Today,* the article by Stephen Board "Fact and Faith in Modern Theology" in the May 26,

1967, issue is entered on the index cards FAITH and THEOLOGY as follows:

CTF 5/26/67 p.7-8, Fact&Faith-Mod.Th.

The file folders should be marked to indicate the months and years of the issues that they hold, such as CTF Jan-June 1967 for the folders holding the issues of *Christianity Today* for the first half of 1967.

A Correspondence File, CF, may also be utilized to preserve important correspondence. Letters may be kept in chronological order in manila folders similar to the General File and indexed by subject and by the name of the correspondent, whether person, organization, or institution. Sets of numbers may be set aside to group letters of particular correspondents and the replys.

Other files may be set up as the following: Poem File, PF; Phonograph Record File, PRF; Tape Recording File, TRF; Motion Picture File, MPF; Filmstrip File, FF; Slide Film File, SFF; and Still Picture File, SPF. The Poem File should be set up similar to the Note File. The materials for the other files should be identified carefully with the file symbol and consecutive numbers. The cases or containers would need to be marked for such materials as records, motion picture films, and filmstrips.

The minister may use as many files as he feels necessary, but not so many that there is needless overlapping of files or insufficient material for some. All the materials in the files that he uses should be recorded in the Index, which is the key to his storehouse of information.

VII. INDEXING BY SCRIPTURE

The minister also needs a system of indexing his materials pertaining to various verses of the Bible. This is especially helpful in preparing messages based on verses and passages of scripture. When material is discovered which has exposition of scripture or illustrations of scripture passages, the scripture reference should be recorded as a subject heading at top left hand corner along with other subject headings pertaining to the material. For example, an article explaining the meaning of the Beatitudes in the Sermon on the Mount is given the subject headings MATTHEW 5:3-12 and BEATITUDES. The entry on the scripture reference card for Matthew is made in the fifth column on the front side, since this is the column for references to scripture with chapters ending with five. The scripture verse or verses is followed by the file symbol only. The entry for the above example is as follows:

MATTHEW				
				5:3-12 GF4

Figure 12

All other materials pertaining to verses from chapters 5, 15, and 25 of
Matthew are entered in the same column, such as:

	5:3-12	GF4
	5:3	GF91
	15:32-39	SF10
	5:13	NF61
	25:31-46	SF97
	5:3	NF85

Figure 13

The material should also be indexed on the subject cards of the Index
according to the subject or subjects discussed. In the above example,
the article is indexed on the subject card BEATITUDES.

VIII. CLASSIFYING BOOKS

The minister needs a system of classifying his books and placing them on his bookshelves. In his early years when his library is small he knows where his books are located through familiarity. In his later years he has more difficulty locating his books because his library has increased in size and he may have moved to other fields of service, which necessitated reshelving his materials. Furthermore, he may at times need someone else to locate his materials, and if he uses a filing system, he needs a simple system to identify his bound materials in his files.

The Dewey Decimal Classification of books, which is used in 90 per cent of all school libraries and public libraries, may be adapted for the minister's use by using the general categories. Most libraries have copies of the abridged edition available for use, or this edition may be purchased from bookstores. The system is suitable for use with the Ministers Filing System. At the back of this book the general plan of the classification is given with the ten general categories and the ten subdivisions. A further breakdown of ten subdivisions is also presented for the category of religion, since this division is used most widely by ministers.

The books are classified in the Dewey Decimal Classification according to the subject treated by the author. In the general categories three numbers are assigned for specific subject areas. Additional numbers are added beyond the decimal point for more detailed classification needed in school and public libraries. In addition a letter symbol may be used to identify an author and a particular book, for several books by different authors writing on the same subject may be in the minister's library. For example, the book *Philosophy of Religion* by David Elton Trueblood is a presentation of the essentials of a philosophy of religion. The book falls in the subject classification 201. The symbol for the author and title identification may be composed of the first two letters of the author's last name written in capital letters and the first letter of the title written in small letters, namely, TRp. The articles "a", "an" and "the" are disregarded at the beginning of a title. Therefore, the symbol used to identify the book is as follows:

201 TRp

The symbol may be printed at the bottom of the spine or on the inside of the front or back cover. As an alternative, labels typed with the classification symbol, the author's last name, and the title may also be used on the inside cover in the following manner:

201 TRp
Trueblood
Philosophy of Religion

The books are then placed on the bookshelves in numerical order from the 000's to the 900's. Books with the same Dewey numbers are arranged alphabetically according to the author-title symbol. The shelves may also be labeled. This is needful if the classification number is not printed on the spine (see Figure 14). If no classification system is used, the shelves should be labeled to facilitate the identification of books and other materials.

Figure 14

IX. INDEXING BOUND MATERIALS

If the minister uses a classification system for shelving his books, he may use it to identify them in the Index. Thus if in his reading he discovers a striking statement, an illustration, an outline, or an exposition of scripture which he feels would be of value at some later date, he indexes the material by entering the classification symbol, the page number, and several words that identify the reference. For example, a reference in the book by Elton Trueblood mentioned above is entered as follows:

201 TRp p.54f,Levels of Knowledge

The "f" indicates that the material is also found on the following pages. If the reference is in a bound volume of a periodical, all that is needed is the first letters of the title, the date, the page number, and the identifying words. A reference to an article in the *Christian Herald* called "Rate Your Religious Beliefs" is indexed in the following way:

CH 5/66 p.27f,Rate Rel. Beliefs

Another method of identifying bound materials is to give each book that is indexed a code symbol based on the first word of the title other than an article. A set of book reference cards is needed, one card for each letter of the alphabet. These may be ruled 4 by 6 inch cards, which would fit behind the Index. When material from a particular book is to be indexed, it is given the symbol composed of the first letter of the first word of the title and the number one. If the book *Philosophy of Religion* is the first to be entered on the book reference card "P", it is given the symbol P1. The number "1", the title, the author, the publisher, and the copyright date are entered on the first line. Each new title beginning with the letter "P" receives the next number, namely, P2, P3, etc., and is entered on successive lines on the book reference cards (see Figure 15). Books should be entered on the reference cards only as they are used in connection with the filing system.

These symbols are used to identify the books in the entries recorded in the Index. For example, the entry for the reference to Trueblood's book cited above is as follows:

P1 p.54f, Levels of Knowledge

Thus, one extra step is needed, namely, the identification of the book symbol in the book reference cards. The minister then needs to locate the book on his shelves either through familiarity, through arranging them on the shelves by subject, or through the use of a classification system.

P.			
NO.	TITLE	AUTHOR	PUBLISHER
1	Philosophy of Religion	D. E. Trueblood	Harper, 1957
2	The Preparation of Sermons	A. W. Blackwood	Abingdon,1948
3	Pulpit Pleadings	R. G. Lee	Broadman,1948
4	Preface to Pastoral Theology	S. Hiltner	Abingdon,1958

Figure 15

X. SUBJECT HEADINGS

The minister needs a system of subject headings as a guide to his classification of materials. This gives him uniformity in his system of indexing. Several reference works are available to the minister, providing him with suggestions for subject headings. These include reference Bibles, Bible dictionaries, topical concordances, religious and Bible encyclopedias, English dictionaries, Roget's Thesarus, and Sears List of Subject Headings, available at most libraries. The indexes of the larger works are especially helpful.

A recommended list of subject headings is provided here to guide the minister in setting up his filing system. Proper names are omitted from the list except for a few examples, but should be listed as subject headings in the minister's own system as need arises. This includes names of persons, places, chronological periods, institutions, organizations, ideas or systems, objects, etc. Names of persons should be listed by the last name first.

Several punctuation marks should be used to indicate more specific subject headings grouped together under a general heading. The comma indicates an inverted subject heading, which allows the grouping together of main headings. The noun provides the general heading followed by the comma and an adjective, which indicates the specific category, e.g., HISTORY, MEDIEVAL. The dash indicates a subdivision of the main heading and provides natural divisions of the main division, e.g., BIBLE — CRITICISM. The parentheses may also be used to specify which particular area is indicated, e.g., ELECTION (THEOLOGY).

Several other notations for the index cards only are needful. The "See" reference is needed to point from a subject heading which is not used to one that is used, e.g., NEW BIRTH See REGENERATION. The "See also" is needed to point to other subject headings of similar nature or to related subjects, e.g., CHRISTIAN ETHICS See also SOCIAL ETHICS; SIN. The semicolon is used to separate two or more subject headings following the "See also."

The list of subject headings here is only a suggested arrangement and is far from complete, but it can serve as a guide. Each minister needs to make his own list according to his background and need and according to his type of ministry. He needs to select as subject headings words that are most familiar to him and to cross reference the less familiar expressions. The arrangement of several general categories into subdivisions, such as BAPTISTS, may serve as a guide for similar groups, such as LUTHERANS, METHODISTS, PRESBYTERIANS, etc. The best arrangement for subject headings is to alphabetize the entries letter by letter and word by word, disregarding the type of punctuation.

LIST OF SUBJECT HEADINGS

ACADEMIC FREEDOM
ACCIDENTS
ACOUSTICS
ADAM   See MAN
ADMINISTRATION   See also CHURCH ADMINISTRATION
ADOLESCENCE   See YOUTH
ADOPTION (THEOLOGY)
ADULTS
ADVENT OF CHRIST   See CHRIST — SECOND COMING
ADVERTISING   See also CHURCH PUBLICITY
AGNOSTICISM   See also ATHEISM; SKEPTICISM
ALCOHOLISM
ALTARS, CHRISTIAN
AMBITION   See also ZEAL
AMERICA   See UNITED STATES
AMERICAN BIBLE SOCIETY   See also BIBLE — SOCIETIES
AMUSEMENTS   See RECREATION
ANABAPTISTS
ANGELS
ANGLICAN CHURCH
ANOINTING
ANTHEMNS   See also CHURCH MUSIC
ANTICHRIST   See also SATAN
ANTI-SEMITISM
ANXIETY   See also FEAR
APOCALYPTIC LITERATURE
APOCRYPHAL LITERATURE
APOLOGETICS
APOSTASY
APOSTLES
APOSTLES' CREED   See also CREEDS
APOSTOLIC AGE
APOSTOLIC FATHERS
APOSTOLIC SUCCESSION
ARCHAEOLOGY, BIBLICAL   See BIBLE — ARCHAEOLOGY
ART, CHRISTIAN
ARTICLES OF FAITH   See CONFESSIONS OF FAITH
ASCENSION   See CHRIST — ASCENSION
ASCETICISM
ASSEMBLIES OF GOD
ASSURANCE   See also ETERNAL LIFE; FAITH
ATHEISM   See also AGNOSTICISM; SKEPTICISM
ATOMIC AGE
ATONEMENT   See also SACRIFICE; SALVATION

AUGUSTINE, AURELIUS
AUTHORITY (GOVERNMENT)   See also CHURCH AND STATE
AUTHORITY (RELIGION)   See also BIBLE — AUTHORITY

BAPTISM
BAPTISM, INFANT
BAPTISM OF JESUS   See CHRIST — BAPTISM
BAPTISM OF THE HOLY SPIRIT   See also HOLY SPIRIT
BAPTISMAL REGENERATION
BAPTIST BROTHERHOOD
BAPTIST STUDENT UNION
BAPTIST TRAINING UNION
BAPTIST WORLD ALLIANCE
BAPTISTRIES
BAPTISTS
BAPTISTS, ALABAMA
BAPTISTS, AMERICAN
BAPTISTS — CHURCH AND STATE
BAPTISTS — CHURCH DISCIPLINE
BAPTISTS — CHURCH POLITY
BAPTISTS — CONFESSIONS
BAPTISTS, CONSERVATIVE
BAPTISTS — DOCTRINE
BAPTISTS, ENGLISH
BAPTISTS, FREEWILL
BAPTISTS, GENERAL
BAPTISTS — HISTORY
BAPTISTS — HYMNS
BAPTISTS, MISSIONARY
BAPTISTS — MISSIONS
BAPTISTS, NATIONAL
BAPTISTS — ORDINANCES
BAPTISTS — ORGANIZATIONS
BAPTISTS, PRIMITIVE
BAPTISTS, SOUTHERN
BEATITUDES
BEECHER, HENRY WARD
BELIEF   See FAITH
BELIEVERS
BENEDICTIONS
BEREAVEMENT
BIBLE
BIBLE — ADDRESSES, ESSAYS, LECTURES
BIBLE AND PUBLIC SCHOOLS
BIBLE AND SCIENCE
BIBLE — ANTIQUITIES
BIBLE — ARCHAEOLOGY

BIBLE — AUTHORITY
BIBLE — BIOGRAPHY
BIBLE — CANON
BIBLE — CHRONOLOGY
BIBLE — COVENANTS
BIBLE — CRITICISM
BIBLE — ESCHATOLOGY   See ESCHATOLOGY
BIBLE — ETHICS
BIBLE — EVIDENCES
BIBLE — EXEGESIS
BIBLE — GEOGRAPHY
BIBLE — HERMENEUTICS   See BIBLE — INTERPRETATION
BIBLE — HISTORY
BIBLE — INFALLIBILITY
BIBLE — ILLUSTRATIONS
BIBLE — INSPIRATION
BIBLE — INTERPRETATION
BIBLE — INTRODUCTION
BIBLE — LANGUAGES
BIBLE — LITERARY CHARACTER
BIBLE — MANUSCRIPTS
BIBLE — MIRACLES
BIBLE — MUSIC
BIBLE — NEW TESTAMENT
BIBLE — OLD TESTAMENT
BIBLE — PARABLES
BIBLE — PICTURES
BIBLE — POETRY
BIBLE — PRIESTHOOD
BIBLE — PROPHECY
BIBLE — PSYCHOLOGY
BIBLE — READING
BIBLE — SOCIAL LIFE AND CUSTOMS
BIBLE — SOCIETIES
BIBLE — STORIES
BIBLE — STUDY AND TEACHING
BIBLE — SYMBOLISM AND TYPOLOGY
BIBLE — TEACHING   See BIBLE — STUDY AND TEACHING
BIBLE — THEOLOGY
BIBLE — TRANSLATION
BIBLE — USE
BIBLE — VERSIONS
BIBLIOGRAPHIES
BIGOTRY
BISHOPS
BLESSINGS

BLOOD (THEOLOGY)
BODY (HUMAN)
BODY OF CHRIST See CHURCH
BOOKS
BROTHERHOODS
BUSINESS

CALLING
CALVARY BAPTIST CHURCH, ST. LOUIS, MO.
CAMP MEETINGS See also REVIVALS
CANAAN See PALESTINE
CANON See BIBLE — CANON
CANTATAS
CAPTIVITY
CATECHISMS
CATHEDRALS See CHURCH ARCHITECTURE
CATHOLICISM
CELIBACY See ASCETICISM
CEMETERIES
CEREMONIES
CHAPLAINS
CHARITIES
CHARITY See LOVE
CHILDREN
CHOIRS — ADULT
CHOIRS — CHILDREN
CHOIRS — YOUTH
CHRIST — ASCENSION
CHRIST — ATONEMENT See ATONEMENT
CHRIST — BAPTISM
CHRIST — BIRTH
CHRIST — BURIAL
CHRIST — CRUCIFIXION
CHRIST — DEATH
CHRIST — DEITY
CHRIST — HUMANITY
CHRIST — INCARNATION
CHRIST — INTERCESSION
CHRIST — KENOSIS See CHRIST — INCARNATION
CHRIST — KINGSHIP
CHRIST — LIFE
CHRIST — LORDSHIP
CHRIST — MESSIAHSHIP
CHRIST — MINISTRY
CHRIST — NAMES
CHRIST — PARABLES

CHRIST — PERSON
CHRIST — PRAYERS
CHRIST, PREACHING OF
CHRIST — PRIESTHOOD
CHRIST — PRAYERS
CHRIST — RESURRECTION
CHRIST — SACRIFICE   See ATONEMENT
CHRIST — SECOND COMING
CHRIST — SINLESSNESS
CHRIST — SONSHIP
CHRIST, TEACHING OF
CHRIST — TEACHINGS
CHRIST — VIRGIN BIRTH   See CHRIST — INCARNATION
CHRIST — WORK
CHRISTENING   See BAPTISM
CHRISTIAN ART
CHRISTIAN ATHLETES
CHRISTIAN EDUCATION
CHRISTIAN ETHICS
CHRISTIAN FELLOWSHIP
CHRISTIAN GROWTH
CHRISTIAN LIFE
CHRISTIAN LITERATURE
CHRISTIAN SCIENCE
CHRISTIAN SERVICE
CHRISTIAN TESTIMONY   See also WITNESSING
CHRISTIAN TRAINING
CHRISTIAN YEAR
CHRISTIANITY   See also CHURCH
CHURCH
CHURCH ADMINISTRATION
CHURCH AND EDUCATION
CHURCH AND SOCIETY
CHURCH AND STATE
CHURCH ARCHITECTURE
CHURCH ATTENDANCE
CHURCH BUDGETS
CHURCH BUILDINGS
CHURCH CENSUS
CHURCH COMMITTEES
CHURCH CONSTITUTIONS
CHURCH COUNCILS
CHURCH COVENANTS

CHURCH DEDICATIONS
CHURCH DENOMINATIONS
CHURCH DISCIPLINE
CHURCH EQUIPMENT
CHURCH FINANCE
CHURCH FURNITURE See CHURCH EQUIPMENT
CHURCH GOVERNMENT
CHURCH HISTORY
CHURCH LAW
CHURCH LIBRARIES
CHURCH MEMBERSHIP
CHURCH MUSIC
CHURCH OF CHRIST
CHURCH OFFICERS See also CHURCH GOVERNMENT
CHURCH ORDINANCES
CHURCH PUBLICITY
CHURCH POLITY See CHURCH GOVERNMENT
CHURCH PROGRAM
CHURCH PROMOTION
CHURCH SCHOOLS
CHURCH SERVICES
CHURCH STAFF
CHURCH SURVEYS See CHURCH CENSUS
CHURCH UNITY
CHURCH WORK, CITY
CHURCH WORK, RURAL
CITIZENSHIP
CIVIL RIGHTS
CIVILIZATION
CLERGY See also MINISTERS
COMFORT
COMMANDMENTS See also TEN COMMANDMENTS
COMMUNION See LORD'S SUPPER
COMMUNISM
COMPARATIVE RELIGION
CONDUCT (CHRISTIAN)
CONDUCTING
CONFESSION
CONFESSIONS OF FAITH
CONGREGATION See also CHURCH
CONGREGATIONALISTS
CONSCIENCE
CONSECRATION See DEDICATION
CONTROVERSIES
CONVERSION See also REGENERATION; SALVATION
CONVICTION OF SIN

CONVOCATIONS
COUNCILS See CHURCH COUNCILS
COUNSELING
COURAGE
COURTSHIP See also LOVE; MARRIAGE
COVENANTS See CHURCH COVENANTS; BIBLE — COVENANTS
COVETOUSNESS
CROSS See ATONEMENT
CRUCIFIXION See CHRIST — CRUCIFIXION
CRUSADES
CULTS
CURSE
CYNICISM See also SKEPTICISM

DAY OF ATONEMENT See also ATONEMENT
DEACONESSES
DEACONS
DEATH
DEDICATION
DEISM
DEMOCRACY
DEMONS See also SATAN
DENOMINATIONS See CHURCH DENOMINATIONS
DEPRAVITY See also SIN
DESPAIR
DESTINY
DEVOTIONAL LITERATURE
DISCIPLES OF CHRIST
DISCIPLESHIP
DISCIPLINE
DISCOURAGEMENT
DISCRIMINATION
DISPENSATIONS (THEOLOGY)
DISSENTERS
DIVINATION
DIVORCE
DOCTRINE See THEOLOGY
DRAMA, RELIGIOUS
DRINKING (ALCOHOLIC BEVERAGES)
DRUG ABUSE

EARTH See also CREATION; WORLD
EASTER
ECOLOGY
ECUMENICISM
EDUCATION See also CHRISTIAN EDUCATION
ELDERS

GIVING   See STEWARDSHIP
GNOSTICISM
GOD   See also THEISIM; TRINITY
GOD — ATTRIBUTES
GOD — NAMES
GOD — NATURE
GOD — SOVEREIGNTY
GOD — WORKS
GODS   See also MYTHOLOGY
GOLDEN RULE
GOODNESS
GOSPEL
GOVERNMENT   See also CHURCH GOVERNMENT
GRACE
GREAT COMMISSION   See also MISSIONS
GUILT   See also SIN

HABITS
HAPPINESS   See also JOY
HATRED
HEATHENISM
HEALING   See also MEDICINE
HEALTH
HEART (SPIRITUAL)
HEAVEN
HELL
HEREDITY
HERESY
HIGHER CRITICISM   See also BIBLE — CRITICISM; LIBERALISM
HISTORY   See also BIBLE — HISTORY
HOLIDAYS
HOLINESS   See SANCTIFICATION
HOLY DAYS   See CHRISTIAN YEAR
HOLY LAND   See PALESTINE
HOLY SPIRIT   See also TRINITY
HOLY WEEK
HOME   See also FAMILY
HONESTY
HOPE
HUMILITY
HUMOR
HYMNODY   See also CHURCH MUSIC
HYMNS   See also CHURCH MUSIC

ICONOCLASM
IDOLATRY
ILLITERACY

ILLNESS, MENTAL
ILLNESS, PHYSICAL
IMAGE OF GOD   See also MAN
IMAGINATION
IMMERSION   See BAPTISM
IMMORALITY
IMMORTALITY   See also ETERNAL LIFE
INCARNATION   See CHRIST — INCARNATION
INDIFFERENCE
INFANT BAPTISM   See BAPTISM, INFANT
INFLUENCE
INQUISITION   See also HERESY; PERSECUTION
INSPIRATION, BIBLICAL   See BIBLE — INSPIRATION
INTEGRATION
INTERBIBLICAL PERIOD
INTERCESSION   See also PRAYER
INTERMEDIATE STATE   See ESCHATOLOGY
INTERPRETATION, BIBLICAL   See BIBLE — INTERPRETATION
INTELLECTUALISM
INVITATION (CHURCH SERVICES)
ISRAEL   See also JUDAISM

JESUS CHRIST   See CHRIST — PERSON
JEWS   See JUDAISM
JOY
JUDAISM
JUDGMENT
JUSTICE
JUSTIFICATION
JUVENILE DELINQUENCY

KINDNESS
KINGDOM OF GOD
KNOWLEDGE

LABOR
LAITY
LANGUAGE
LAST DAYS   See ESCHATOLOGY
LAW
LAW OF GOD   See also COMMANDMENTS;
    TEN COMMANDMENTS
LAYMEN   See also LAITY
LAZINESS
LEADERSHIP
LEARNING

LENT
LIBERALISM   See also MODERNISM
LIBERTY   See also CIVIL RIGHTS; RELIGIOUS LIBERTY
LIBRARIES
LIFE
LIGHT
LITERATURE   See also CHRISTIAN LITERATURE
LITURGIES
LORD'S PRAYER
LORD'S SUPPER
LOVE
LOVE, CHRISTIAN
LOVE OF GOD
LOYALTY
LUTHERANS

MAN   See also CREATION
MARRIAGE
MARTYRDOM   See also PERSECUTION
MEDICINE AND RELIGION
MEDITATIONS   See also DEVOTIONAL LITERATURE
MENTAL HEALTH
MERCY
METHODISTS
MILLENNIUM   See ESCHATOLOGY
MIND
MINISTERS   See also CLERGY; PASTORS
MINISTERS — CALLING
MINISTERS — CHARACTER
MINISTERS — EDUCATION
MINISTERS — LICENSING
MINISTERS OF EDUCATION
MINISTERS OF MUSIC
MINISTERS — ORDINATION
MINISTERS — SERVICE
MINISTER'S WIFE
MINISTRY
MIRACLES
MISSIONARIES
MISSIONS
MISSIONS — AFRICA
MISSIONS, ASSOCIATIONAL
MISSIONS, CITY
MISSIONS, FOREIGN
MISSIONS, HOME
MISSIONS, MEDICAL
MISSIONS, STATE

MODERATION
MODERNISM   See also LIBERALISM
MONASTICISM
MONEY   See also STEWARDSHIP
MONOTHEISM   See also GOD
MORALITY
MUSIC   See also BIBLE — MUSIC; CHURCH MUSIC
MYSTERIES (THEOLOGY)
MYSTICISM
MYTHOLOGY

NAMES
NATURE
NAZARENES
NEGROES
NEO-ORTHODOXY
NEW BIRTH   See REGENERATION
NEW TESTAMENT   See BIBLE — NEW TESTAMENT
NEWSPAPERS
NONCONFORMISTS
NUNS

OBEDIENCE
OBITUARIES
OFFERINGS
OLD AGE
OLD TESTAMENT   See BIBLE — OLD TESTAMENT
OPTIMISM
ORATORIOS
ORATORY
ORDER OF WORSHIP
ORDINANCES   See CHURCH ORDINANCES
ORDINATION   See MINISTERS — ORDINATION
ORGAN MUSIC
ORGANS
ORPHANS AND ORPHANAGES
ORTHODOX CHURCHES

PACIFISM
PAGANISM
PALESTINE
PANTHEISM
PAPACY
PARABLES
PARISHES
PARLIMENTARY PROCEDURE
PAROCHIAL SCHOOLS

PASTORAL CARE
PASTORAL PSYCHOLOGY
PASTORAL THEOLOGY
PASTORS   See also CLERGY; MINISTERS
PATIENCE
PATRIOTISM
PEACE
PENTATEUCH
PENTECOST
PENTECOSTALISM
PERSECUTION
PERSEVERANCE OF THE SAINTS   See also ETERNAL SECURITY
PERSONALITY
PHILOSOPHY
PHILOSOPHY OF RELIGION
PIANO MUSIC
PIANOS
PIETISM
POETRY
POLEMICS
POLITICS
POLYTHEISM
POPES   See PAPACY
POPULATION
POVERTY
POWER, SPIRITUAL
PRACTICAL THEOLOGY
PRAISE   See also CHURCH MUSIC
PRAYER
PRAYER MEETING
PRAYERS
PREACHERS   See also EVANGELISTS; MINISTERS; PASTORS
PREACHING   See also SERMONS
PREACHING — CONTENT
PREACHING — DELIVERY
PREACHING — HISTORY
PREACHING — PREPARATION
PREACHING — STYLE
PREDESTINATION   See also ELECTION
PREJUDICE   See also DISCRIMINATION
PRESBYTERIANS
PRIDE
PRIESTHOOD

PRIESTHOOD OF BELIEVERS
PRIESTS
PROCRASTINATION
PROFESSION OF FAITH
PROPHECY
PROPHETS
PROTESTANTS
PROVIDENCE OF GOD   See also GOD — WORKS
PSALMNODY   See also CHURCH MUSIC
PSALTERS
PSYCHIATRY AND RELIGION   See also MEDICINE AND
    RELIGION
PSYCHOLOGY, BIBLICAL
PSYCHOLOGY, PASTORAL
PSYCHOLOGY OF RELIGION
PUBLIC RELATIONS
PUBLIC SCHOOLS
PUBLICITY   See also CHURCH PUBLICITY
PULPIT COMMITTEES
PUNISHMENT   See also JUDGMENT
PURITANS

QUOTATIONS

RACE RELATIONS
RADIO
RATIONALISM
REASON   See also MIND
RECONCILIATION   See also ATONEMENT
RECREATION
REDEDICATION   See DEDICATION
REDEMPTION   See also ATONEMENT; SALVATION
REFORMATION, THE
REFORMED CHURCH
REGENERATION
RELIGION
RELIGIONS
RELIGIOUS EDUCATION
RELIGIOUS LIBERTY
REPENTANCE   See also CONVERSION
RESURRECTION   See also CHRIST — RESURRECTION
REVELATION   See also BIBLE — INSPIRATION
REVERENCE
REVIVALS   See also EVANGELISM
RHETORIC
RIGHTEOUSNESS
RITUAL

SABBATH   See also SUNDAY
SACRAMENTS   See also CHURCH ORDINANCES
SACRIFICE   See also ATONEMENT
SAINTS
SALVATION   See also ATONEMENT; CONVERSION;
     REDEMPTION
SANCTIFICATION   See also DEDICATION
SATAN
SCIENCE AND RELIGION
SECOND COMING   See CHRIST — SECOND COMING
SECTS   See also CHURCH DENOMINATIONS
SEGREGATION
SERMON ILLUSTRATIONS
SERMON ON THE MOUNT
SERMONS   See also PREACHING
SEX AND RELIGION
SICKNESS
SIN   See also DEPRAVITY; FALL OF MAN; GUILT
SINGING — CONGREGATIONAL
SINGING, STUDY OF
SISTERHOODS
SKEPTICISM   See also AGNOSTICISM; ATHEISM
SLAVERY
SMOKING
SOCIAL ETHICS   See ETHICS, SOCIAL
SOCIALISM AND CHRISTIANITY
SONGS (SACRED)   See also CHURCH — MUSIC
SONSHIP
SOUL
SOUL WINNING   See also EVANGELISM; WITNESSING
SPEAKING IN TONGUES
SPIRIT
SPIRIT OF GOD   See HOLY SPIRIT
SPIRITS, EVIL   See DEMONS; SATAN
SPIRITUAL LIFE
STEALING
STEWARDS
STEWARDSHIP
STUDY
SUFFERING
SUICIDE
SUNDAY   See also SABBATH
SUNDAY SCHOOLS
SUPERSTITION
SYMBOLISM
SYMPATHY

SYNAGOGUES

TABERNACLE, THE
TEACHERS
TEACHING   See also EDUCATION; CHRISTIAN EDUCATION
TELEVISION
TEMPERANCE
TEMPLE, THE
TEMPTATION
TEN COMMANDMENTS
TESTIMONY   See CHRISTIAN TESTIMONY
THANKSGIVING
THEISM   See also GOD
THEOLOGIANS
THEOLOGY
THEOLOGY, BIBLICAL
THEOLOGY, PASTORAL
THEOLOGY, SYSTEMATIC
TITHING   See also CHURCH FINANCING; STEWARDSHIP
TOLERANCE
TRACTS, RELIGIOUS
TRADITION, RELIGIOUS
TRINITY   See also GOD
TRUST   See FAITH
TRUSTEES
TRUTH   See also WORD OF GOD
TYPOLOGY

UNBELIEF
UNION WITH CHRIST   See also SPIRITUAL LIFE
UNITARIANISM
UNITED STATES
UNITY, CHURCH
UNIVERSE   See CREATION
UNIVERSITIES AND COLLEGES
UNPARDONABLE SIN
UNSAVED PEOPLE

VACATION BIBLE SCHOOLS
VIRGIN BIRTH   See CHRIST — INCARNATION
VISITATION, CHURCH   See also ENLISTMENT, CHURCH
VOCATIONAL GUIDANCE   See also COUNSELING

WAR
WEALTH
WEDDINGS   See also MARRIAGE
WILL
WILL OF GOD

WILLS
WISDOM
WITNESSING   See also SOUL WINNING
WOMAN'S MISSIONARY UNION
WOMEN
WORD OF GOD
WORK
WORKS
WORLD   See also CREATION
WORSHIP
WORSHIP, FAMILY
WRITING

YOUTH
YOUTH MOVEMENTS

ZEAL

DEWEY DECIMAL CLASSIFICATION

GENERAL SUMMARY

000	**GENERAL WORKS**		**500**	**PURE SCIENCE**
010	Bibliography		510	Mathematics
020	Library Science		520	Astronomy
030	General Encyclopedias		530	Physics
040	General Collected Essays		540	Chemistry
050	General Periodicals		550	Earth Sciences
060	General Societies		560	Paleontology
070	Newspapers Journalism		570	Anthropology & Biology
080	Collected Works		580	Botanical Sciences
090	Manuscripts & Rare Books		590	Zoological Sciences
100	**PHILOSOPHY**		**600**	**TECHNOLOGY**
110	Metaphysics		610	Medical Sciences
120	Metaphysical Theories		620	Engineering
130	Branches of Psychology		630	Agriculture
140	Philosophical Topics		640	Home Economics
150	General Psychology		650	Business
160	Logic		660	Chemical Technology
170	Ethics		670	Manufactures
180	Ancient & Medieval Philosophy		680	Other Manufactures
190	Modern Philosophy		690	Building Construction
200	**RELIGION**		**700**	**THE ARTS**
210	Natural Theology		710	Landscape & Civic Art
220	Bible		720	Architecture
230	Doctrinal Theology		730	Sculpture
240	Devotional & Practical		740	Drawing & Decorative Arts
250	Pastoral Theology		750	Painting
260	Christian Church		760	Engraving
270	Christian Church History		770	Photography
280	Christian Churches & Sects		780	Music
290	Other Religions		790	Recreation
300	**SOCIAL SCIENCES**		**800**	**LITERATURE**
310	Statistics		810	American
320	Political Science		820	English
330	Economics		830	German
340	Law		840	French
350	Public Administration		850	Italian
360	Social Welfare		860	Spanish
370	Education		870	Latin
380	Public Services & Utilities		880	Greek
390	Customs & Folklore		890	Other Literature
400	**LANGUAGE**		**900**	**HISTORY**
410	Comparative		910	Geography, Travel, & Description
420	English		920	Biography
430	German		930	Ancient History
440	French		940	Europe
450	Italian		950	Asia
460	Spanish		960	Africa
470	Latin		970	North America
480	Greek		980	South America
490	Other Languages		990	Pacific Islands

DEWEY DECIMAL CLASSIFICATION

RELIGION

200 RELIGION
201   Philosophy & Theories
202   Handbooks & Outlines
203   Dictionaries & Encyclopedias
204   Essays & Lectures
205   Periodicals
206   Organizations & Societies
207   Study & Teaching
208   Collections
209   History

210 NATURAL THEOLOGY
211   Knowledge of God
212   Pantheism
213   Creation of Universe
214   Theodicy
215   Religion & Science
216   Good & Evil
217   Worship
218   Immortality
219   Analogy

220 BIBLE
221   Old Testament
222   Historical Books
223   Poetic Books
224   Prophetic Books
225   New Testament
226   Gospels & Acts
227   Epistles
228   Revelation
229   Apocrypha

230 DOCTRINAL THEOLOGY
231   God
232   Christology
233   Man
234   Salvation
235   Angels, Devils, Satan
236   Eschatology
237   Future State
238   Christian Creeds
239   Apologetics

240 DEVOTIONAL & PRACTICAL
241   Moral Theology
242   Meditations
243   Evangelistic Writings
244   Miscellany
245   Hymnology
246   Christian Symbolism
247   Sacred Furniture & Vestments
248   Personal Religion
249   Family Worship

250 PASTORAL THEOLOGY
251   Preaching (Homiletics)
252   Sermons
253   Pastor
254   Church & Parish Administration
255   Brotherhoods & Sisterhoods
256   Societies for Parish Work
257   Parish Education Work
258   Parish Welfare Work
259   Other Parish Work

260 CHRISTIAN CHURCH
261   Christian Social Theology
262   Government & Organization
263   Sabbath, Lord's Day, & Sunday
264   Public Worship, Ritual, & Liturgy
265   Sacraments & Ordinances
266   Missions
267   Religious Associations
268   Religious Education & Sunday Schools
269   Revivals & Spiritual Renewal

270 CHRISTIAN CHURCH HISTORY
271   Religious Orders
272   Persecutions
273   Heresies
274   In Europe
275   In Asia
276   In Africa
277   In North America
278   In South America
279   In Other Parts of the World

280 CHRISTIAN CHURCHES & SECTS
281   Primitive & Oriental Churches
282   Roman Catholic Church
283   Anglican Churches
284   Protestantism
285   Presbyterian & Congregational Churches
286   Baptist & Immersionist Churches
287   Methodist Churches
288   Unitarian Church
289   Other Christian Sects

290 OTHER RELIGIONS
291   Comparative Religion
292   Greek & Roman
293   Teutonic & Norse Religions
294   Brahmanism & Buddhism
295   Zorastrianism & Related
296   Judaism
297   Islam & Bahaism
298
299   Other Non-Christian Religions